God

A Play in One Act

by Woody Allen

A SAMUEL FRENCH ACTING EDITION

SAMUEL FRENCH

FOUNDED 1830

SAMUELFRENCH.COM

CAST

ACTOR
WRITER
GIRL
DORIS
MAID
TRICHINOSIS
PROMPTER
BURSITIS
MAN *(In Audience)*
LORENZO MILLER
WOMAN *(In Audience)*
BLANCHE DUBOIS
DIABETES
PHIDIPIDES *(A Slave, played by* DIABETES*)*
ANOTHER GREEK SLAVE
MASTER
BOB
WENDY
GUARD
WOMAN *(On Stage)*
KING
DOCTOR
WESTERN UNION DELIVERY BOY
STANLEY
ANOTHER MAN *(In Audience)*
ANOTHER WOMAN *(In Audience)*
GREEK CHORUS
GOD *(Non-speaking Role)*
GROUCHO MARX *(Non-speaking Role)*

SCENE: Athens. Approximately 500 B.C. Two distraught Greeks in the center of enormous empty amphitheater. Sunset. One is the ACTOR; the other, the WRITER. They are both thinking and distracted. They should be played by two good, broad burlesque clowns.

ACTOR

Nothing . . . just nothing . . .

WRITER

What?

ACTOR

Meaningless. It's empty.

WRITER

The ending.

ACTOR

Of course. What are we discussing? We're discussing the ending.

WRITER

We're always discussing the ending.

ACTOR

Because it's hopeless.

WRITER

I admit it's unsatisfying.

ACTOR

Unsatisfying!? It's not even believable. The trick is to start

at the ending when you write a play. Get a good strong
ending and then write backwards.

                    WRITER
I've tried that. I got a play with no beginning.

                    ACTOR
That's absurd.

                    WRITER
Absurd? What's absurd?

                    ACTOR
Every play must have a beginning, middle, and end.

                    WRITER
Why?

                    ACTOR
                 (Confidently)
Because everything in nature has a beginning, middle, and
end.

                    WRITER
What about a circle?

                    ACTOR
                   (Thinks)
Okay . . . A circle has no beginning, middle, or end—but
they're not much fun either.

                    WRITER
Diabetes, think of an ending. We open in three days.

                    ACTOR
Not me. I'm not opening in this turkey. I have a reputation
as an actor, a following . . . My public expects to see me in
a suitable vehicle.

                    WRITER
May I remind you, you're a starving, out-of-work actor

whom I've generously consented to let appear in my play in an effort to assist your comeback.

ACTOR

Starving, yes . . . Out of work, perhaps . . . Hoping for a comeback, maybe—but a drunkard?

WRITER

I never said you were a drunkard.

ACTOR

Yes, but I'm also a drunkard.

WRITER
(In a fit of sudden inspiration)
What if your character ripped a dagger from his robes and in a fit of frenzied frustration, tore away at his own eyes until he blinded himself?

ACTOR

Yeah, it's a great idea. Have you eaten anything today?

WRITER

What's wrong with it?

ACTOR

It's depressing. The audience will take one look at it and—

WRITER

I know—make that funny sound with their lips.

ACTOR

It's called hissing.

WRITER

Just once I want to win the competition! Once, before my life is over, I want my play to take first prize. And it's not the free case of ouzo I care about, it's the honor.

ACTOR
(Suddenly inspired)

What if the king suddenly changed his mind? There's a
positive idea.

                              WRITER
He'd never do it.

                              ACTOR
                     (Selling him on it)
If the queen convinced him?

                              WRITER
She wouldn't. She's a bitch.

                              ACTOR
But if the Trojan Army surrendered—

                              WRITER
They'd fight to the death.

                              ACTOR
Not if Agamemnon reneged on his promise?

                              WRITER
It's not in his nature.

                              ACTOR
But I could suddenly take up arms and make a stand.

                              WRITER
It's against your character. You're a coward—an insignifi-
cant wretched slave with the intelligence of a worm. Why
do you think I cast you?

                              ACTOR
I've just given you six possible endings!

                              WRITER
Each more clumsy than the last.

                              ACTOR
It's the play that's clumsy.

WRITER

Human beings don't behave that way. It's not in their nature.

ACTOR

What does their nature mean? We're stuck with a hopeless ending.

WRITER

As long as man is a rational animal, as a playwright, I cannot have a character do anything on stage he wouldn't do in real life.

ACTOR

May I remind you that we don't exist in real life.

WRITER

What do you mean?

ACTOR

You are aware that we're characters in a play right now in some Broadway theater? Don't get mad at me, I didn't write it.

WRITER

We're characters in a play and soon we're going to see my play . . . which is a play within a play. And they're watching us.

ACTOR

Yes. It's highly metaphysical, isn't it?

WRITER

Not only is it metaphysical, it's stupid!

ACTOR

Would you rather be one of them?

WRITER
(Looking at the audience)

Definitely not. Look at them.

ACTOR

Then let's get on with it!

WRITER
(Mutters)

They paid to get in.

ACTOR

Hepatitis, I'm talking to you!

WRITER

I know, the problem is the ending.

ACTOR

It's always the ending.

WRITER
(Suddenly to the audience)

Do you folks have any suggestions?

ACTOR

Stop talking to the audience! I'm sorry I mentioned them.

WRITER

It's bizarre, isn't it? We're two ancient Greeks in Athens and we're about to see a play I wrote and you're acting in, and they're from Queens or some terrible place like that and they're watching us in someone else's play. What if they're characters in another play? And someone's watching them? Or what if nothing exists and we're all in somebody's dream? Or, what's worse, what if only that fat guy in the third row exists?

ACTOR

That's my point. What if the universe is not rational and people are not set things? Then we could change the ending and it wouldn't have to conform to any fixed notions. You follow me?

WRITER

Of course not. (To the audience) You follow him? He's an actor. Eats at Sardi's.

ACTOR

Play characters would have no determined traits and could
choose their own characters. I wouldn't have to be the slave
just because you wrote it that way. I could choose to become
a hero.

WRITER

Then there's no play.

ACTOR

No play? Good, I'll be at Sardi's.

WRITER

Diabetes, what you're suggesting is chaos!

ACTOR

Is freedom chaos?

WRITER

Is freedom chaos? Hmm . . . That's a toughie. *(To the
audience)* Is freedom chaos? Did anybody out there major in
philosophy?
(A GIRL from the audience answers)

GIRL

I did.

WRITER

Who's that?

GIRL

Actually I majored in gym, with a philosophy minor.

WRITER

Can you come up here? .

ACTOR

What the hell are you doing?

GIRL

Does it matter if it was Brooklyn College?

WRITER

Brooklyn College? No, we'll take anything.
(She's made her way up)

ACTOR

I am really pissed off!

WRITER

What's eating you?

ACTOR

We're in the middle of a play. Who is she?

WRITER

In five minutes the Athenian Drama Festival begins, and I
have no ending for my play!

ACTOR

So?

WRITER

Serious philosophical questions have been raised. Do we
exist? Do they exist? *(Meaning the audience)* What is the true
nature of human character?

GIRL

Hi. I'm Doris Levine.

WRITER

I'm Hepatitis and this is Diabetes. We're ancient Greeks.

DORIS

I'm from Great Neck.

ACTOR

Get her off this stage!

WRITER
*(Really looking her up
and down, as she's lovely)*

She's very sexy.

ACTOR

What has that got to do with it?

DORIS

The basic philosophical question is: If a tree falls in the forest and no one is around to hear it—how do we know it makes a noise?
(Everyone looks around, puzzled over this)

ACTOR

Why do we care? We're on Forty-fifth Street.

WRITER

Will you go to bed with me?

ACTOR

Leave her alone!

DORIS
(To ACTOR)

Mind your own business.

WRITER
(Calling offstage)

Can we lower the curtain here? Just for five minutes . . . *(To the audience)* Sit there. It'll be a quickie.

ACTOR

This is outrageous! It's absurd! *(To DORIS)* Do you have a friend?

DORIS

Sure. *(Calling to the audience)* Diane, you want to come up here . . . I got something going with a couple of Greeks. *(No response)* She's shy.

ACTOR

Well, we have a play to do. I'm going to report this to the author.

WRITER

I *am* the author!

ACTOR

I mean the original author.

WRITER
(Sotto voce to the ACTOR)
Diabetes, I think I can score with her.

ACTOR

What do you mean, score? You mean intercourse—with all these people watching?

WRITER

I'll lower the curtain. Some of them even do it. Not many, probably.

ACTOR

You idiot, you're fictional, she's Jewish—you know what the children will be like?

WRITER

Come on, maybe we can get her friend up here.
(The ACTOR goes to stage left to use the telephone)
Diane? This is a chance for a date with ————. *(Uses a real actor's name)* He's a big actor . . . lots of TV commercials . . .

ACTOR
(Into the phone)
Get me an outside line.

DORIS

I don't want to cause any trouble.

WRITER

It's no trouble. It's just that we've seemed to have lost touch with reality here.

DORIS

Who knows what reality really is?

WRITER

You're so right, Doris.

DORIS

(Philosophically)

So often people think they grasp reality when what they're really responding to is "fakeositude."

WRITER

I have an urge toward you that I'm sure is real.

DORIS

Is sex real?

WRITER

Even if it's not, it's still one of the best fake activities a person can do.

(He grabs her, she pulls back)

DORIS

Don't. Not here.

WRITER

Why not?

DORIS

I don't know. That's my line.

WRITER

Have you ever made it with a fictional character before?

DORIS

The closest I came was an Italian.

ACTOR

(He's on the phone. We hear the party on other end through a filter)

Hello?

PHONE
(Maid's voice)

Hello, Mr. Allen's residence.

ACTOR

Hello, may I speak to Mr. Allen?

MAID'S VOICE

Who's calling, please?

ACTOR

One of the characters in his play.

MAID

One second. Mr. Allen, there's a fictional character on the phone.

ACTOR
(To the others)

Now we'll see what happens with you lovebirds.

WOODY'S VOICE

Hello.

ACTOR

Mr. Allen?

WOODY

Yes?

ACTOR

This is Diabetes.

WOODY

Who?

ACTOR

Diabetes. I'm a character you created.

WOODY

Oh, yes . . . I remember, you're a badly drawn character . . . very one-dimensional.

ACTOR

Thanks.

WOODY

Hey—isn't the play on now?

ACTOR

That's what I'm calling about. We got a strange girl up on the stage and she won't get off and Hepatitis is suddenly hot for her.

WOODY

What does she look like?

ACTOR

She's pretty, but she doesn't belong.

WOODY

Blonde?

ACTOR

Brunette . . . long hair.

WOODY

Nice legs?

ACTOR

Yes.

WOODY

Good breasts?

ACTOR

Very nice.

WOODY

Keep her there, I'll be right over.

ACTOR

She's a philosophy student. But she's got no real answers . . . typical product of the Brooklyn College cafeteria.

WOODY

That's funny, I used that line in *Play It Again, Sam* to describe a girl.

ACTOR

I hope it got a better laugh there.

WOODY

Put her on.

ACTOR

On the phone?

WOODY

Sure.

ACTOR
(To DORIS)

It's for you.

DORIS
(Whispers)

I've seen him in the movies. Get rid of him.

ACTOR

He wrote the play.

DORIS

It's pretentious.

ACTOR
(Into the phone)

She won't speak to you. She says your play is pretentious.

WOODY

Oh, Jesus. Okay, call me back and let me know how the play ends.

ACTOR

Right.
(He hangs up, then does a double take, realizing what the author said)

DORIS

Can I have a part in your play?

ACTOR

I don't understand. Are you an actress or a girl playing an actress?

DORIS

I always wanted to be an actress. Mother hoped I'd become a nurse. Dad felt I should marry into society.

ACTOR

So what do you do for a living?

DORIS

I work for a company that makes deceptively shallow serving dishes for Chinese restaurants.
(A Greek enters from the wings)

TRICHINOSIS

Diabetes, Hepatitis. It's me, Trichinosis. *(Ad-lib greetings)* I have just come from a discussion with Socrates at the Acropolis and he proved that I didn't exist, so I'm upset. Still, word has it you need an ending for your play. I think I have just the thing.

WRITER

Really?

TRICHINOSIS

Who's she?

DORIS

Doris Levine.

TRICHINOSIS

Not from Great Neck?

DORIS

Yes.

TRICHINOSIS

You know the Rappaports?

DORIS

Myron Rappaport?

TRICHINOSIS
(Nodding)
We both worked for the Liberal party.

DORIS

What a coincidence.

TRICHINOSIS

You had an affair with Mayor Lindsay.

DORIS

I wanted to—he wouldn't.

WRITER

What's the ending?

TRICHINOSIS

You're much prettier than I imagined.

DORIS

Really?

TRICHINOSIS

I'd like to sleep with you right now.

DORIS

Tonight's my night. *(TRICHINOSIS takes her wrist passionately)* Please. I'm a virgin. Is that my line?
(The PROMPTER with book peeks out from the wings; is wearing a sweater)

PROMPTER

"Please. I'm a virgin." Yes.
(Exits)

WRITER

What's the goddamn ending?

TRICHINOSIS

Huh? Oh— *(Calls off)* Fellas!
(Some Greeks wheel out an elaborate machine)

WRITER

What the hell is that?

TRICHINOSIS

The ending for your play.

ACTOR

I don't understand.

TRICHINOSIS

This machine, which I've spent six months designing in my
brother-in-law's shop, holds the answer.

WRITER

How?

TRICHINOSIS

In the final scene—when all looks black, and Diabetes the
humble slave is in a position most hopeless—

ACTOR

Yes?

TRICHINOSIS

Zeus, Father of the Gods, descends dramatically from on
high and brandishing his thunderbolts, brings salvation to a
grateful but impotent group of mortals.

DORIS

Deus ex machina.

TRICHINOSIS

Hey—That's a great name for this thing!

DORIS

My father works for Westinghouse.

WRITER

I still don't get it.

TRICHINOSIS

Wait'll you see this thing in action. It flies Zeus in. I'm going to make a fortune with this invention. Sophocles put a deposit on one. Euripides wants two.

WRITER

But that changes the meaning of the play.

TRICHINOSIS

Don't speak till you see a demonstration. Bursitis, get into the flying harness.

BURSITIS

Me?

TRICHINOSIS

Do what I say. You won't believe this.

BURSITIS

I'm afraid of that thing.

TRICHINOSIS

He's kidding . . . Go ahead, you idiot, we're on the verge of a sale. He'll do it. Ha, ha . . .

BURSITIS

I don't like heights.

TRICHINOSIS

Get into it! Hurry up. Let's go! Get into your Zeus suit! A demonstration.
(Exiting as BURSITIS protests)

BURSITIS

I want to call my agent.

WRITER

But you're saying God comes in at the end and saves everything.

ACTOR

I love it! It gives the people their money's worth!

DORIS

He's right. It's like those Hollywood Bible movies.

WRITER

(Taking center stage a little too dramatically)

But if God saves everything, man is not responsible for his actions.

ACTOR

You wonder why you're not invited to more parties . . .

DORIS

But without God, the universe is meaningless. Life is meaningless. We're meaningless. *(Deadly pause)* I have a sudden and overpowering urge to get laid.

WRITER

Now I'm not in the mood.

DORIS

Really? Would anyone in the audience care to make it with me?

ACTOR

Stop that! *(To the audience)* She's not serious, folks.

WRITER

I'm depressed.

ACTOR

What's bothering you?

WRITER

I don't know if I believe in God.

DORIS
(To the audience)
I am serious.

ACTOR
If there's no God, who created the universe?

WRITER
I'm not sure yet.

ACTOR
Who do you mean, you're not sure yet!? When are you going to know?

DORIS
Anybody out there want to sleep with me?

MAN
(Rising in the audience)
I'll sleep with that girl if nobody else will.

DORIS
Will you, sir?

MAN
What's wrong with everybody? A beautiful girl like that? Aren't there any red-blooded men in the audience? You're all a bunch of New York left-wing Jewish intellectual commie pinkos—
(LORENZO MILLER comes out from wings. He is dressed in contemporary clothes)

LORENZO
Sit down, will you sit down?

MAN
Okay, okay.

WRITER
Who are you?

LORENZO

Lorenzo Miller. I created this audience. I'm a writer.

WRITER

What do you mean?

LORENZO

I wrote: a large group of people from Brooklyn, Queens, Manhattan, and Long Island come to the Golden Theater and watch a play. There they are.

DORIS
(Pointing to the audience)
You mean they're fictional too? *(LORENZO nods)* They're not free to do as they please?

LORENZO

They think they are, but they always do what's expected of them.

WOMAN
(Suddenly a WOMAN rises in audience, quite angrily)
I'm not fictional!

LORENZO

I'm sorry, madam, but you are.

WOMAN

But I have a son at the Harvard Business School.

LORENZO

I created your son; he's fictional. Not only is he fictional, he's homosexual.

MAN

I'll show you how fictional I am. I'm leaving this theater and getting my money back. This is a stupid play. In fact, it's no play. I go to the theater, I want to see something with a story—with a beginning, middle, and end—instead of this bullshit. Good night.
(Exits up the aisle in a huff)

LORENZO
(To the audience)
Isn't he a great character. I wrote him very angry. Later he feels guilty and commits suicide. *(Sound: gunshot)* Later!

MAN
(Reenters with a smoking pistol)
I'm sorry, did I do it too soon?

LORENZO
Get out of here!

MAN
I'll be at Sardi's.
(Exits)

LORENZO
(In the audience, dealing with various people of the actual audience)
What's your name, sir? Uh-huh. *(Ad-lib section, depending on what audience says)* Where are you from? Isn't he cute? Great character. Must remind them to dress him differently. Later this woman leaves her husband for this guy. Hard to believe, I know. Oh—look at this guy. Later he rapes that lady.

WRITER
It's terrible being fictional. We're all so limited.

LORENZO
Only by the limits of the playwright. Unfortunately you happen to have been written by Woody Allen. Think if you were written by Shakespeare.

WRITER
I don't accept it. I'm a free man and I don't need God flying in to save my play. I'm a good writer.

DORIS
You want to win the Athenian Drama Festival, don't you?

WRITER

(Suddenly dramatic)

Yes. I want to be immortal. I don't want to just die and be forgotten. I want my works to live on long after my physical body has passed away. I want future generations to know I existed! Please don't let me be a meaningless dot, drifting through eternity. I thank you, ladies and gentlemen. I would like to accept this Tony Award and thank David Merrick . . .

DORIS

I don't care what anybody says, I'm real.

LORENZO

Not really.

DORIS

I think, therefore I am. Or better yet, I *feel*—I have an orgasm.

LORENZO

You do?

DORIS

All the time.

LORENZO

Really?

DORIS

Very frequently.

LORENZO

Yes?

DORIS

Most of the time I do, yes.

LORENZO

Yes?

DORIS

At least half the time.

LORENZO

No.

DORIS

I do! With certain men . . .

LORENZO

Hard to believe.

DORIS

Not necessarily through intercourse. Usually it's oral—

LORENZO

Uh-huh.

DORIS

Of course I fake it too. I don't want to insult anybody.

LORENZO

Have you ever had an orgasm?

DORIS

Not really. No.

LORENZO

Because none of us are real.

WRITER

But if we're not real, we can't die.

LORENZO

No. Not unless the playwright decides to kill us.

WRITER

Why would he do something like that?
(From the wings, BLANCHE DuBOIS enters)

BLANCHE

Because, sugar, it satisfies something called their—aesthetic
sensibility.

WRITER

(All turn to look at her)

Who are you?

BLANCHE

Blanche. Blanche DuBois. It means "white woods." Don't get up, please—I was just passing through.

DORIS

What are you doing here?

BLANCHE

Seeking refuge. Yes—in this old theater . . . I couldn't help overhearing your conversation. Could I get a coke with a little bourbon in it?

ACTOR

(Appears. We didn't realize he'd slipped away)

Is a Seven-Up okay?

WRITER

Where the hell were you?

ACTOR

I went to the bathroom.

WRITER

In the middle of the play?

ACTOR

What play? *(To BLANCHE)* Will you explain to him we're all limited.

BLANCHE

I'm afraid it's all too true. Too true and too ghastly. That's why I ran out of my play. Escaped. Oh, not that Mr. Tennessee Williams is not a very great writer, but honey— he dropped me in the center of a nightmare. The last thing I remember, I was being taken out by two strangers, one who held a strait jacket. Once outside the Kowalski residence, I broke free and ran. I've got to get into another play, a play where God exists . . . somewhere where I can rest at last. That's why you must put me in your play and allow Zeus, young and handsome Zeus to triumph with his thunderbolt.

WRITER

You went to the bathroom?

TRICHINOSIS
(Enters)

Ready for the demonstration.

BLANCHE

A demonstration. How wonderful.

TRICHINOSIS
(Calling offstage)

Ready out there? Okay. It's the end of the play. Everything looks hopeless for the slave. All other means desert him. He prays. Go ahead.

ACTOR

Oh, Zeus. Great god. We are confused and helpless mortals. Please be merciful and change our lives. *(Nothing happens)* Er . . . great Zeus . . .

TRICHINOSIS

Let's go, fellas! For Christ's sake.

ACTOR

Oh, great God.
(Suddenly there is thunder and fabulous lightning. The effect is wonderful: ZEUS descends, hurling thunderbolts majestically)

BURSITIS
(As ZEUS)

I am Zeus, God of Gods! Worker of miracles! Creator of the universe! I bring salvation to all!

DORIS

Wait'll Westinghouse sees this!

TRICHINOSIS

Well, Hepatitis, what do you think?

WRITER

I love it! It's better than I expected. It's dramatic, it's flamboyant. I'm going to win the festival! I'm a winner. It's so religious. Look, I got chills! Doris!

(He grabs her)

DORIS

Not now.

(There is a general exit, a light change . . .)

WRITER

I must do some immediate rewrites.

TRICHINOSIS

I'll rent you my God machine for twenty-six fifty an hour.

WRITER

(To LORENZO)

Can you introduce my play?

LORENZO

Sure, go ahead. *(THEY all exit. LORENZO stays behind and faces audience. As he speaks, a Greek CHORUS enters and sits in the background of the amphitheater. White-robed, naturally)* Good evening and welcome to the Athenian Drama Festival. *(Sound: cheering)* We got a great show for you tonight. A new play by Hepatitis of Rhodes, entitled, "The Slave." *(Sound: cheers)* Starring Diabetes as the slave, with Bursitis as Zeus, Blanche DuBois, and Doris Levine from Great Neck. *(Cheers)* The show is brought to you by Gregory Londos' Lamb Restaurant, just opposite the Parthenon. Don't be a Medusa with snakes in *your* hair when you're looking for a place to dine out. Try Gregory Londos' Lamb Restaurant. Remember, Homer liked it—and he was blind.

(He exits. DIABETES plays the slave named PHIDIPIDES and right now, he drifts on with another GREEK SLAVE as the CHORUS takes over)

CHORUS
Gather round, ye Greeks, and heed the story of Phidipides —one so wise, so passionate, so steeped in the glories of Greece.

DIABETES
My point is, what are we going to do with such a big horse?

FRIEND
But they want to give it to us for nothing.

DIABETES
So what? Who needs it? It's a big wooden horse . . . What the hell are we going to do with it? It's not even a pretty horse. Mark my words, Cratinus—as a Greek statesman, I would never trust the Trojans. You notice they never take a day off?

FRIEND
Did you hear about Cyclops? He got a middle eye infection.

VOICE OFF
Phidipides! Where is that slave?

DIABETES
Coming, Master!

MASTER
(Enters)
Phidipides—there you are. There's work to be done. The grapes need picking, my chariot must be repaired, we need water from the well—and you're out shmoozing.

DIABETES
I wasn't shmoozing, Master, I was discussing politics.

MASTER

A slave discussing politics! Ha, ha!

CHORUS

Ha, ha . . . That's rich.

DIABETES

I'm sorry, Master.

MASTER

You and the new Hebrew slave clean the house. I'm expecting guests. Then get on with all the other tasks.

DIABETES

The new Hebrew?

MASTER

Doris Levine.

DORIS

You called?

MASTER

Clean up. Let's go. Hurry on.

CHORUS

Poor Phidipides. A slave. And like all slaves, he longed for one thing.

DIABETES

To be taller.

CHORUS

To be free.

DIABETES

I don't want to be free.

CHORUS

No?

DIABETES

I like it this way. I know what's expected of me. I'm taken

care of. I don't have to make any choices. I was born a slave
and I'll die a slave. I have no anxiety.

CHORUS

Boo . . . boo . . .

DIABETES

Ah, what do you know, chorus boys.
(He kisses DORIS, she pulls away)

DORIS

Don't.

DIABETES

Why not? Doris, you know my heart is heavy with love—or
as you Hebrews are fond of saying, I have a thing for you.

DORIS

It can't work.

DIABETES

Why not?

DORIS

Because you like being a slave and I hate it. I want my
freedom. I want to travel and write books, live in Paris,
maybe start a woman's magazine.

DIABETES

What's the big deal about freedom? It's dangerous. To
know one's place is safe. Don't you see, Doris, governments
change hands every week, political leaders murder one
another, cities are sacked, people are tortured. If there's a
war, who do you think gets killed? The free people. But
we're safe because no matter who's in power, they all need
someone to do the heavy cleaning.
(He grabs her)

DORIS

Don't. While I am still a slave I can never enjoy sex.

DIABETES

Would you be willing to fake it?

DORIS

Forget it.

CHORUS

And then one day the fates lent a hand.
(The FATES enter, a couple dressed like American tourists, wearing jazzy Hawaiian shirts; BOB has a camera around his neck)

BOB

Hi, we're the Fates, Bob and Wendy Fate. We need someone to take an urgent message to the king.

DIABETES

The king?

BOB

You would be doing mankind a great service.

DIABETES

I would?

WENDY

Yes, but it's a dangerous mission, and even though you are a slave, you may say no.

DIABETES

No.

BOB

But it will give you a chance to see the palace in all its glory.

WENDY

And the reward is your freedom.

DIABETES

My freedom? Yes, well, I'd love to help you, but I have a roast in the stove.

DORIS

Let me do it.

BOB

It's too dangerous for a woman.

DIABETES

She's a very fast runner.

DORIS

Phidipides, how can you refuse?

DIABETES

When you're a coward, certain things come easy.

WENDY

We beg of you—please—

BOB

The fate of mankind hangs in the balance.

WENDY

We'll raise the reward. Freedom for you and any person of your choice.

BOB

Plus a sixteen-piece starter set of silverware.

DORIS

Phidipides, here's our chance.

CHORUS

Go ahead, you jerk.

DIABETES

A dangerous mission followed by personal freedom? I'm getting nauseous.

WENDY

(Hands him an envelope)

Take this message to the king.

DIABETES

Why can't you take it?

BOB

We're leaving for New York in a few hours.

DORIS

Phidipides, you say you love me—

DIABETES

I do.

CHORUS

Let's go, Phidipides, the play is bogging down.

DIABETES

Decisions, decisions . . . *(The phone rings, and he answers it)*
Hello?

WOODY'S VOICE

Will you take the goddamn message to the king. We'd all
like to get the hell out of here.

DIABETES
(Hangs up)
I'll do it. But only because Woody asked me to.

CHORUS
(Sings)
Poor Professor Higgins—

DIABETES

That's the wrong show, you idiots!

DORIS

Good luck, Phidipides.

WENDY

You're really going to need it.

DIABETES

What do you mean?

WENDY

Bob here is really a practical joker.

DORIS

After we're free we can go to bed, and maybe for once I'll enjoy it.

HEPATITIS
(Pops on stage)

Sometimes a little grass before you make it—

ACTOR

You're the writer!

HEPATITIS

I couldn't resist!

(Exit)

DORIS

Go!

DIABETES

I'm going!

CHORUS

And so Phidipides set out on his journey, bearing an important message for King Oedipus.

DIABETES

King Oedipus?

CHORUS

Yes.

DIABETES

I hear he lives with his mother.
(Effects: Wind and lightning as SLAVE trudges on)

CHORUS

Over deep mountains, through high valleys.

DIABETES

High mountains and deep valleys. Where did we get this chorus?

CHORUS

At all times at the mercy of the Furies.

DIABETES

The Furies are having dinner with the Fates. They went to Chinatown. The Hong Fat Noodle Company.

HEPATITIS
(Enters)

Sam Wo's is better.

DIABETES

There's always a line at Sam Wo's.

CHORUS

Not if you ask for Lee. He'll seat you, but you have to tip him.

(HEPATITIS exits)

DIABETES
(Proudly)

Yesterday I was a lousy slave, never having ventured beyond my master's property. Today I carry a message to the king, the king himself. I see the world. Soon I'll be a free man. Suddenly human possibilities are opening up to me. And because of it—I have an uncontrollable urge to throw up. Oh, well . . .

(Wind)

CHORUS

Days turn into weeks, weeks into months. Still Phidipides struggles on.

DIABETES

Can you turn off the goddamn wind machine?

CHORUS

Poor Phidipides, mortal man.

DIABETES

I'm tired, I'm weary, I'm sick. I can't go on. My hand is
shaking . . . (The CHORUS begins humming a slow version of
"Dixie") All around me men dying, war and misery, brother
against brother; the South, rich in tradition; the North,
mostly industrial. President Lincoln, sending the Union
Army to destroy the plantation. The Old Homestead.
Cotton—comin' down the river . . . (HEPATITIS enters and
stares at him) Lawsy, lawsy, Miss Eva—Ah can't cross the
ice. It's General Beauregard and Robert E. Lee . . . Ah—
(Notices HEPATITIS staring at him) I—I . . . I got carried
away.
(HEPATITIS grabs him around the neck and pulls him to the side)

HEPATITIS

C'mere! What the hell are you doing!?

DIABETES

Where's the palace? I'm walking around for days! What
kind of play is this!? Where the hell is the goddamn palace?
In Bensonhurst?

HEPATITIS

You're at the palace if you'd stop ruining my play! Guard!
Come on now, shape up.
(A powerful GUARD enters)

GUARD

Who are you?

DIABETES

Phidipides.

GUARD

What brings you to the palace?

DIABETES

The palace? I'm here?

GUARD

Yes. This is the royal palace. The most beautiful structure in all of Greece, marble, majestic, and completely rent-controlled.

DIABETES

I bear a message for the king.

GUARD

Oh, yes. He is expecting you.

DIABETES

My throat is parched and I have not eaten in days.

GUARD

I will summon the king.

DIABETES

What about a roast-beef sandwich?

GUARD

I will get the king and a roast-beef sandwich. How do you want that?

DIABETES

Medium.

GUARD

(Takes out a pad and writes)

One medium. You get a vegetable with that.

DIABETES

What do you have?

GUARD

Let's see, today . . . carrots or baked potato.

DIABETES

I'll have the baked potato.

GUARD

Coffee?

DIABETES

Please. And a toasted bow tie—if you have one—and the king.

GUARD

Right. *(As he exits)* Let me have an RB to go with a regular coffee.

(The FATES cross, taking pictures)

BOB

How do you like the palace?

DIABETES

I love it.

BOB
(Handing his wife the camera)
Take one of us together.
(As she does)

DIABETES

I thought you two were going back to New York.

WENDY

You know how fate is.

BOB

Unreliable. Take it easy.

DIABETES
(Leans in to smell the flower in BOB's lapel)
That's a pretty flower.
(Gets an eyeful of water as FATES laugh)

BOB

I'm sorry, I couldn't resist.
(Offers his hand. DIABETES shakes it. Gets a shock from a joy buzzer)

DIABETES

Ahhhh!
(FATES exit laughing)

WENDY

He loves to play tricks on people.

DIABETES

(To CHORUS)

You knew he was out to get me.

CHORUS

He's a scream.

DIABETES

Why didn't you warn me?

CHORUS

We don't like to get involved.

DIABETES

You don't like to get involved? You know, a woman was stabbed to death on the BMT while sixteen people looked on and didn't help.

CHORUS

We read it in the *Daily News*, and it was the IRT.

DIABETES

If one person had the guts to help her, maybe she'd be here today.

WOMAN

(Enters with knife in her chest)

I am here.

DIABETES

I had to open my mouth.

WOMAN

A woman works her whole life on DeKalb Ave. I'm reading the *Post*, six hooligans—dope addicts—grab me and throw me down.

CHORUS

There weren't six, there were three.

WOMAN

Three, six—they had a knife, they wanted my money.

DIABETES

You should have given it to them.

WOMAN

I did. They still stabbed me.

CHORUS

That's New York. You give 'em the money and they still stab you.

DIABETES

New York? It's everywhere. I was walking with Socrates in downtown Athens, and two youths from Sparta jump out from behind the Acropolis and want all our money.

WOMAN

What happened?

DIABETES

Socrates proved to them using simple logic that evil was merely ignorance of the truth.

WOMAN

And?

DIABETES

And they broke his nose.

WOMAN

I just hope your message for the king is good news.

DIABETES

I hope so, for his sake.

WOMAN

For your sake.

DIABETES

Right and—what do you mean, for my sake?

CHORUS
(Derisively)

Ha, ha, ha!
(The light becomes more ominous)

DIABETES

The light is changing . . . What is that? What happens if
it's bad news?

WOMAN

In ancient times, when a messenger brought a message to
the king, if the news was good, the messenger received a
reward.

CHORUS

Free passes to the Loew's Eighty-sixth Street.

WOMAN

But if the news was bad . . .

DIABETES

Don't tell me.

WOMAN

The king would have the messenger put to death.

DIABETES

Are we in ancient times?

WOMAN

Can't you tell by what you're wearing?

DIABETES

I see what you mean. Hepatitis!

WOMAN

Sometimes the messenger would have his head cut off . . . if
the king was in a forgiving mood.

DIABETES

A forgiving mood, he cuts your head off?

CHORUS

But if the news is really bad—

WOMAN

Then the messenger is roasted to death—

CHORUS

Over a slow fire.

DIABETES

It's been so long since I've been roasted over a slow fire, I can't remember if I like it or not.

CHORUS

Take our word for it—you won't like it.

DIABETES

Where's Doris Levine? If I get my hands on that Hebrew slave from Great Neck . . .

WOMAN

She can't help you, she's miles away.

DIABETES

Doris! Where the hell are you?

DORIS
(In the audience)

What do you want?

DIABETES

What are you doing there?

DORIS

I got bored with the play.

DIABETES

What do you mean, you got bored? Get up here! I'm up to my ass in trouble because of you!

DORIS
(Coming up)

I'm sorry, Phidipides, how did I know what happened in ancient history? I studied philosophy.

DIABETES

If the news is bad, I die.

DORIS

I heard her.

DIABETES

Is this your idea of freedom?

DORIS

Win a couple, lose a couple.

DIABETES

Win a couple, lose a couple? That's what they teach you at Brooklyn College?

DORIS

Hey, man, get off my back.

DIABETES

If the news is bad I'm finished. Wait a minute! The news! The message. I got it right here! (*Fumbles, takes a message from an envelope. Reads*) For Best Supporting Actor, the winner is —————. (*Use the name of the actor playing HEPATITIS*)

HEPATITIS
(*Pops on*)

I want to accept this Tony Award and thank David Merrick—

ACTOR

Get off, I read the wrong message!
(*Pulls out the real one*)

WOMAN

Hurry, the king's coming.

DIABETES

See if he has my sandwich.

DORIS

Hurry, Phidipides!

DIABETES
(Reads)

The message is one word.

DORIS

Yes?

DIABETES

How'd you know?

DORIS

Know what?

DIABETES

What the message is, it's "yes."

CHORUS

Is that good or bad?

DIABETES

Yes? Yes is affirmative? No? Isn't it? *(Testing it)* *Yes!*

DORIS

What if the question is, Does the queen have the clap?

DIABETES

I see your point.

CHORUS

His majesty, the king!
(Fanfare, big entrance of KING)

DIABETES

Sire, does the queen have the clap?

KING

Who ordered this roast beef?

DIABETES

I did, sire. Is that carrots? Because I asked for a baked potato.

KING

We're out of baked potatoes.

DIABETES

Then take it back. I'll go across the street.

CHORUS

The message. *(DIABETES keeps* shh*ing them)* The message, he has the message.

KING

Humble slave, do you have a message for me?

DIABETES

Humble king, er , . . yes, as a matter of fact . . .

KING

Good.

DIABETES

Can you tell me the question?

KING

First the message.

DIABETES

No, you first.

KING

No, you.

DIABETES

No, you.

KING

No, you.

CHORUS

Make Phidipides go first.

KING

Him?

CHORUS

Yes.

KING

How can I?

CHORUS

Shmuck, you're the king.

KING

Of course, I'm the king. What is the message?
(The GUARD draws a sword)

DIABETES

The message is . . . ye-no—*(Trying to get an idea before spilling it)* no-yeah—maybe—maybe—

CHORUS

He's lying.

KING

The message, slave.
(The GUARD puts a sword to DIABETES' throat)

DIABETES

It is one word, sire.

KING

One word?

DIABETES

Amazing, isn't it, because for the same money he's allowed fourteen words.

KING

A one-word answer to my question of questions. Is there a god?

DIABETES

That's the question?

KING

That—is the only question.

DIABETES

(Looks at DORIS, relieved)

Then I'm proud to give you the message. The word is yes.

KING

Yes?

DIABETES

Yes.

CHORUS

Yes.

DORIS

Yes.

DIABETES

Your turn.

WOMAN

(Lisp)

Yeth.

(DIABETES gives her an annoyed look)

DORIS

Isn't that fabulous!

DIABETES

I know what you're thinking, a little reward for your faithful messenger—but our freedom is more than enough—on the other hand, if you insist on showing your appreciation, I think diamonds are always in good taste.

KING

(Gravely)

If there is a god, then man is not responsible and I will surely be judged for my sins.

DIABETES

Pardon me?

KING

Judged for my sins, my crimes. Very horrible crimes, I am doomed. This message you bring me dooms me for eternity.

DIABETES

Did I say yes? I meant no.

GUARD

(Seizes the envelope and reads the message)
The message is yes, sire.

KING

This is the worst possible news.

DIABETES

(Dropping to his knees)
Sire, it's not my fault. I'm a lowly messenger, I don't create the message. I merely transmit it. It's like her majesty's clap.

KING

You will be torn apart by wild horses.

DIABETES

I knew you'd understand.

DORIS

But he's only the messenger. You can't have him torn apart by wild horses. You usually roast them over a slow fire.

KING

Too good for this scum!

DIABETES

When the weatherman predicts rain, do you kill the weatherman?

KING

Yes.

DIABETES

I see. Well. I'm dealing with a schizophrenic.

KING

Seize him.
(The GUARD does)

DIABETES

Wait, sire. A word in my defense.

KING

Yes?

DIABETES

This is only a play.

KING

That's what they all say. Give me your sword. I want the
pleasure of this kill myself.

DORIS

No, no—oh, why did I get us into this?

CHORUS

Don't worry, you're young, you'll find somebody else.

DORIS

That's true.

KING
(Raises the sword)

Die!

DIABETES

Oh, Zeus—God of Gods, come forward with your thunderbolt and save me— *(All look up; nothing happens, awkward
moment)* Oh, Zeus . . . Oh, Zeus!!!

KING

And now—die!

DIABETES

Oh, Zeus—where the hell is Zeus!

HEPATITIS
(He enters and looks up)
For Christ's sake, let's go with the machine! Lower him!

TRICHINOSIS
(Enters from the other side)
It's stuck!

DIABETES
(Giving the cue again)
Oh, great Zeus!

CHORUS
All men come to the same end.

WOMAN
I'm not gonna stand here and let him get stabbed like I was
on the BMT!

KING
Grab her.
(The GUARD grabs her and stabs her)

WOMAN
That's twice this week! Son of a bitch.

DIABETES
Oh, great Zeus! God, help me!
*(Effect. Lightning—ZEUS is lowered very clumsily and he jerks
around until we see the lowering wire has strangled him. Everyone
looks on, stunned)*

TRICHINOSIS
Something's wrong with the machine! It's out of joint.

CHORUS

At last, the entrance of God!
(But he's definitely dead)

DIABETES

God . . . God? God? God, are you okay? Is there a doctor
in the house?

DOCTOR
(In the audience)

I'm a doctor.

TRICHINOSIS

The machine got screwed up.

HEPATITIS

Psst. Get off. You're ruining the play.

DIABETES

God is dead.

DOCTOR

Is he covered by anything?

HEPATITIS

Ad-lib.

DIABETES

What?

HEPATITIS

Ad-lib the ending.

TRICHINOSIS

Somebody pulled the wrong lever.

DORIS

His neck is broken.

KING
(Trying to continue the play)

Er . . . well, messenger . . . see what you've done.
(Brandishes the sword. DIABETES grabs it)

DIABETES
(Grabbing sword)
I'll take that.

KING
What the hell are you doing?

DIABETES
Kill me, eh? Doris, get over here.

KING
Phidipides, what are you doing?

GUARD
Hepatitis, he's ruining the end.

CHORUS
What're you doing, Phidipides? The king should kill *you.*

DIABETES
Says who? Where is it written? No—I choose to kill the king.
(Stabs the KING, but the sword is fake)

KING
Leave me alone . . . He's crazy . . . Stop! . . . That tickles.

DOCTOR
(Taking the pulse of the body of GOD)
He's definitely dead. We better move him.

CHORUS
We don't want to get involved.
(THEY start exiting, carrying GOD off)

DIABETES
The slave decides to be a hero!
(Stabs the GUARD; the sword is still a fake)

GUARD
What the hell are you doing?

DORIS

I love you, Phidipides. *(He kisses her.)* Please, I'm not in the mood.

HEPATITIS

My play . . . my play! *(To CHORUS)* Where are you going?

KING

I'm going to call my agent at the William Morris Agency. Sol Mishkin. He'll know what to do.

HEPATITIS

This is a very serious play with a message! If it falls apart, they'll never get the message.

WOMAN

The theater is for entertainment. There's an old saying, if you want to send a message, call Western Union.

WESTERN UNION DELIVERY BOY
(Enters on a bicycle)

I have a telegram for the audience. It's the author's message.

DIABETES

Who's he?

DELIVERY BOY
(Dismounts, sings)

Happy birthday to you, happy birthday to you—

HEPATITIS

It's the wrong message!

DELIVERY BOY
(Reads the wire)

I'm sorry, here it is. God is dead. Stop. You're on your own. And it's signed—The Moscowitz Billiard Ball Company?

DIABETES

Of course anything is possible. I'm the hero now.

DORIS

And I just know I'm going to have an orgasm. I know it.

DELIVERY BOY
(Still reads)

Doris Levine can definitely have an orgasm. Stop. If she wants to. Stop.

(He grabs her)

DORIS

Stop.
(In the background a brutish man enters)

STANLEY

Stella! Stella!

HEPATITIS

There is no more reality! Absolutely none.
(GROUCHO MARX runs across stage chasing BLANCHE. A MAN in audience rises)

MAN

If anything's possible, I'm not going home to Forest Hills! I'm tired of working on Wall Street. I'm sick of the Long Island Expressway!
(Grabs a WOMAN in the audience. Rips her blouse off, chases her up the aisle. This could also be an usherette)

HEPATITIS

My play . . . *(The characters have left the stage, leaving the two original characters, the author and actor, HEPATITIS and DIABE-TES)* My play . . .

DIABETES

It was a good play. All it needed was an ending.

HEPATITIS

But what did it mean?

DIABETES

Nothing . . . just nothing . . .

HEPATITIS

What?

DIABETES

Meaningless. It's empty.

HEPATITIS

The ending.

DIABETES

Of course. What are we discussing? We're discussing the ending.

HEPATITIS

We're always discussing the ending.

DIABETES

Because it's hopeless.

HEPATITIS

I admit it's unsatisfying.

DIABETES

Unsatisfying!? It's not even believable. *(The lights start dimming)* The trick is to start at the ending when you write a play. Get a good, strong ending, and then write backwards.

HEPATITIS

I've tried that. I got a play with no beginning.

DIABETES

That's absurd.

HEPATITIS

Absurd? What's absurd?

(BLACKOUT)